# Star Ledger

T0108915

Winner of the
EDWIN FORD PIPER
Poetry Award

*Publication of this book
was made possible
with the generous assistance of
Janet Piper*

Poems by Lynda Hull

# Star Ledger

University of Iowa Press    Iowa City

University of Iowa Press, Iowa City 52242
Copyright © 1991 by Lynda Hull
Printed in the United States of America

Design by Richard Hendel

Printed on acid-free paper

Library of Congress Cataloging-in-Publication Data

Hull, Lynda, 1954–
Star ledger/poems by Lynda Hull.—1st ed.
p.     cm.—(Edwin Ford Piper poetry award)
ISBN 0-87745-319-5
I. Title.  II. Series.
PS3558.U397487  1991          90-49398
811'.54—dc20          CIP

01  00  99  98  97  96  95  P  7  6  5  4  3

*In memory of Mary Green Hull*

# Acknowledgments

Acknowledgment is made to the following journals where certain of these poems first appeared: *Agni Review*: "Black Mare," "Magical Thinking," "Midnight Reports," "Visiting Hour"; *Boulevard*: "Gateway to Manhattan"; *Denver Quarterly*: "Fairy Tales: Steel Engravings"; *Gettysburg Review*: "Adagio"; *Indiana Review*: "Studies from Life"; *Kenyon Review*: "Lost Fugue for Chet," "Carnival"; *Missouri Review*: "Counting in Chinese"; *New England Review/Bread Loaf Quarterly*: "Aubade"; *North American Review*: "Vita Brevis"; *Pequod*: "Frugal Repasts"; *Poetry*: "Shore Leave," "Utopia Parkway"; *Poetry Miscellany*: "Cubism, Barcelona"; *Provincetown Arts*: "The Real Movie, with Stars"; *Quarterly West*: "Utsuroi," "The Crossing, 1927."

Several of these poems have also been included in anthologies: "Black Mare" in *Under 35: The New Generation* (Doubleday); "Hospice" in *Poets for Life: Seventy-Six Poets Respond to AIDS* (Crown) and in *Pushcart Prize XV* (Pushcart Press); "Frugal Repasts," "Love Song during Riot with Many Voices," and "Shore Leave" in *New American Poets of the 90's* (David R. Godine).

I would like to thank the National Endowment for the Arts for a fellowship which allowed me to complete this book and the Yaddo and Edna St. Vincent Millay colonies for fruitful residencies.

"Love Song during Riot with Many Voices" is for Dean Young and

Cornelia Nixon; "The Real Movie, with Stars" is for Ralph Angel; "Adagio" is for Mark Doty; and "Abacus" is for soul-sister Barbara Anderson. "The Crossing, 1927" makes use of passages from Edna St. Vincent Millay's journals and is for Herbert Morris. "Utsuroi" owes a debt to Marina Warner. Most of all my best thanks to David, whose constant support and belief made this book possible.

# Contents

★ III ★

*How perilous to choose not
to love the life we're shown.*
Seamus Heaney

★ I ★

Almost time to dress for the sun's total eclipse
   so the child pastes one last face
in her album of movie stars – Myrna Loy
   and Olivia de Havilland – names meant to conjure
sultry nights, voluptuous turns across
   some dance floor borne on clouds. Jean Harlow.

Clipped from the Newark evening paper, whole galaxies
   of splendid starlets gaze, fixed to violet pages
spread drying on the kitchen table. The child whispers
   their names when she tests "lorgnettes"
made that morning out of shirtboards, old film
   negatives gleaned from her grandmother's hat box.

Through phony opera glasses, hall lights blur
   stained sepia above her, and her grandmother's
room is stained by a tall oak's crown, yellow
   in the window. Acorns crack against asphalt
three floors down. The paper promised
   "a rare conjunction of sun and moon and earth."

Her grandmother brushed thick gray hair.
   Cut glass bottles and jewel cases.
Above the corset her back was soft, black moles
   she called her "melanomas" dusted across

powdery skin like a night sky, inside out.
    The Spanish fan dangles from her wrist

and when she stands she looks like an actress
    from the late-night movies. The child sifts
costume brooches, glass rubies and sapphires,
    to find the dark gold snake ring with emerald chips
for eyes. She carries the miniature hourglass
    to the sagging porch, then waiting turns it over

and over. Uncertain in high heels, she teeters
    and the shawl draped flamenco-style keeps sliding off
her shoulder, so she glances up the block to Girl Scouts
    reeling down the flag. The child hates their dull uniforms,
how they scatter shrieking through leafsmoke and the sheen
    of fallen chestnuts. She touches the ring, heavy

on a ribbon circling her neck, then thinks she'll sew
    the album pages with green embroidery silk.
Her grandmother snaps the fan and they raise lorgnettes
    to the sun's charcoaled face, its thin wreath
of fire. Quiet, the Girl Scouts bow their heads – sleek
    Italian ones and black girls with myriad tight braids.

Streetlights hum on, then the towers of Manhattan flare
    beyond the river. The earth must carve its grave ellipse

through desert space, through years and histories
  before it will cross with sun and moon this way again.
Minor starlets in the child's album will fade and tatter,
  fleeting constellations with names flimsy as

the shawl that wraps her shoulders. She'll remember this
  as foolish. The girls by the flag will mostly leave
for lives of poverty, crippled dreams, and Newark
  will collapse to burn like another dying star.
But none of this has happened. Afternoon has stilled
  with the eclipse that strips them of their shadows,

so each one stands within their own brief human orbit
  while the world reverses, then slowly, recovers.

She wears the sailor suit – a blouse with anchors,
skirt puffed in stiff tiers above her thin
knees, those spit-shined party shoes. Behind her
a Cadillac's fabulous fins gleam and reflected
in the showroom window, her father's a mirage.
The camera blocks his face as he frames
a shot that freezes her serious grin,
the splendid awkwardness of almost-adolescence.
He's all charm with the car dealer and fast-talks
them a test-drive in a convertible like the one
on display, a two-tone Coupe de Ville. But once
around the corner he lowers the top and soon
they're fishtailing down dump-truck paths,
the Jersey Meadows smoldering with trash fires.
He's shouting *Maybelline, why can't you be true,*
and seagulls lift in a tattered curtain across
Manhattan's hazy skyline. Dust-yellow clouds
behind him, he's handsome as a matinee idol,
wavy hair blown straight by sheer velocity.
Tall marsh weeds bend, radiant as her heart's
relentless tide. They rip past gaping Frigidaires,
rusted hulks of cranes abandoned to the weather.
Her father teases her she's getting so pretty
he'll have to jump ship sometime and take her
on a real whirl, maybe paint the whole town red.
For her *merchant marine* conjures names like

condiments – Malabar, Marseilles – places where
the laws of gravity don't hold. She can't believe
her father's breakneck luck will ever run out.
He accelerates and spins out as if the next thrill
will break through to some more durable joy.
So she stands, hands atop the windshield and shouts
the chorus with him, and later when they drop the car
he takes her to a cocktail bar and plays Chuck Berry
on the jukebox. She perches on a barstool and twirls
her Shirley Temple's paper umbrella, watches
the slick vinyl disks stack up, rhythms collecting,
breaking like surf as her father asks the barmaid
to dance with him through "Blue Moon," then foamy
glass after glass of beer. The barmaid's sinuous
in red taffeta, a rhinestone choker around
her throat. Her father's forgotten her and dances
a slow, slow tango in the empty bar and the dark
comes on like the tiny black rose on the barmaid's
shoulder rippling under her father's hand.
The girl thinks someday she'll cover her skin
with roses, then spins, dizzy on the barstool.
She doesn't hear the woman call her foolish
mortal father a two-bit trick because she's whirling
until the room's a band of light continuous
with the light the city's glittering showrooms throw
all night long over the sleek, impossible cars.

Dusk after dusk, through the smoke of industry
and autumn buffed across the sky, the shy girl
loses herself in books her grandmother once read
as a child. Blue and violet spines shine

in her hands, gilt-edged pages and those stories
of runaway children transformed to sea urchins
caught by underwater journeys. At some point
in her mind, the Thames and Hudson braid their waters

and below, the traffic flows like the river flows
across the pages, steely, engraved with whorls
and the salesgirls wave from curbs and bus-stop
islands like good children left behind, sketched

on riverbanks or sleeping the sleep
of a different century. The playground cries
of Catholic girls across the street filter
through the curtains to her reading chair

and although they surely know the soul
is a white, clear room they carry with them, they
seem so purely physical, unbound in blue gym suits,
cool air stippling their skin. Nuns' faces

from sidelines float, bodiless, the girl believes,
on columns of air, their habits shirring the wind.
The girl looks back to her book and her grandmother's
humming through a clatter of enamelware and radio news

from Cuba, then the Aqueduct race results –
Fred Caposella chanting a spell of Caribbean jockeys'
names steaming through the alarm of garlic
and rosemary that clouds the panes of London

where yellow squares of gaslight show the way
home to solitary walkers draped in bracelets,
thin collars of fog. Beyond the parlor windows
the girl sees women turn in heavy silks through

brittle rings of gossip that rise up the stairwell
to the empty nursery, an open window where
their children have descended ladders of white mist,
and it's too late to call them home from the river's

quick current. Already the bridges have closed
over them, arms embracing, letting go
those children whose bodies swiftly grow
strange, paradisal. Book open on her lap, the girl's

already in love with promises of transport. She traces
the caps of engraved sea-leaves that frame those faces
like sunflowers turning to follow the moon's silver
imperative that lays a ruler across the waves, the tides

where her story begins in the surge and lapse of traffic.
She hears *Bay of Pigs* then *Odds 10 to 1*, and the cries
fading, now turning sharper across the street as if
by sheer volume, each girl might stay her departure.

# ★ Love Song during Riot with Many Voices ★

Newark, 1967

The bridge's iron mesh chases pockets of shadow
and pale through blinds shuttering the corner window

to mark this man, this woman, the young eclipse
their naked bodies make – black, white, white,
black, the dying fall of light rendering bare walls

incarnadine, color of flesh and blood occluded

in voices rippling from the radio: Saigon besieged,
Hanoi, snipers and the riot news helicoptered
from blocks away. All long muscle, soft

hollow, crook of elbow bent sequined above the crowd,
nightclub dancers farandole their grind and slam
into streets among the looters. Let's forget the 58¢

lining his pockets, forget the sharks and junkyards

within us. Traffic stalls to bricks shattering,
the windows, inside her, bitch I love you, city breaking
down and pawnshops disgorge their contraband of saxophones

and wedding rings. Give me a wig, give me
a pistol. Hush baby, come to papa, let me hold you

through night's broken circuitry, chromatic
and strafed blue with current. Let's forget this bolt
of velvet fallen from a child's arm brocading

pavement where rioters careen in furs and feathered hats
burdened with fans, the Polish butcher's strings

of sausages, fat hams. This isn't a lullaby a parent
might croon to children before sleep, but all of it
belongs: in the station torn advertisements whisper
easy credit, old men wait for any train out of town

and these lovers mingling, commingling their bodies,
this slippage, a haul and wail of freight trains

pulling away from the yards. With this girl
I'll recall black boys by the soda shop, other times
with conked pompadours and scalloped afterburns
stenciled across fenders. Through the radio

Hendrix butanes his guitar to varnish, crackle
and discord of "Wild Thing." Sizzling strings,
that Caravaggio face bent to ask the crowd

did they want to see him sacrifice something
he loved. Thigh, mouth, breast, small of back, dear

hollow of the throat, don't you understand this pressure

of hotbox apartments? There's no forgetting the riot
within, fingernails sparking to districts
rivering with flame. What else could we do

but cling and whisper together as children after
the lullaby is done, but no, never as children, never

do they so implore, oh god, god, bend your dark visage

over this acetylene skyline, over Club Zanzibar
and the Best of Three, limed statues in the parks, over
the black schoolgirl whose face is smashed again

and again. No journalist for these aisles of light
the cathedral spots cast through teargas and the mingling,
commingling of sisters' voices in chapels, storefront
churches asking for mercy.

                   Beyond the bridge's
iron mesh, the girl touches a birthmark
behind her knee and wishes the doused smell
of charred buildings was only hydrants flushing hot concrete.

Summertime. Pockets of shadow and pale. Too hot
to sleep. Hush baby, come to papa, board
the window before morning's fractured descant,

a staccato crack of fire escapes snapping pavement
and citizens descending, turning back with points of flame

within their eyes before they too must look away.
At dawn, when the first buses leave, their great wipers arc
like women bending through smoke

to burdens, singing terror, singing pity.

That's how billboards give up their promises –
they look right into your window, then whisper
*sex, success*. The Salem girl's smoke plume
marries the gulf between the high-rise projects,
the usual knife's edge ballet enacted nightly there
for the benefit of no one. It's just that
around midnight every love I've known flicks open
like a switchblade and I have to start talking,
talking to drown out the man in the radio
who instructs me I'm on the edge of a new day
in this city of Newark which is not a city

of roses, just one big hockshop. I can't tell you
how it labors with its grilled storefronts, air
rushing over the facts of diamonds, appliances,
the trick carnations. But you already know that.
The M-16 Vinnie sent – piece by piece – from Vietnam
is right where you left it the day you skipped town
with the usherette of the Paradise Triple-X Theater.
You liked the way she played her flashlight down
those rows of men, plaster angels flanked around
that screen. Sometimes you'd go fire rounds over
the landfill, said it felt better than crystal meth,
a hit that leaves a trail of neon, ether.

I keep it clean, oiled, and some nights it seems
like a good idea to simply pick up that rifle
and hold it, because nothing's safe. You know
how it is: one minute you're dancing, the next you're flying
through plate glass and the whole damn town is burning
again with riots and looters, the bogus politicians.
We'd graduated that year, called the city ours,
a real bed of Garden State roses. I've drawn x's
over our eyes in the snapshot Vinnie took commencement
night, a line of x's over our linked hands. The quartet
onstage behind us sang a cappella – four brothers
from Springfield Ave. spinning in sequined tuxedos,

palms outstretched to the crowd, the Latin girls
from Ironbound shimmering in the brief conflagration
of their beauty, before the kids, before
the welfare motels, corridors of cries and exhalations.
I wore the heels you called my blue suede shoes,
and you'd given yourself a new tattoo, my name across
your bicep, in honor of finishing, in honor of the future
we were arrogant enough to think would turn out right.
I was laughing in that picture, laughing when the rain
caught us later and washed the blue dye from my shoes –
blue, the color of bruises, of minor regrets.

The tide foams in with its cargo of debris, and this man,
delirious in evening clothes, kneels begging me *please*

and it doesn't matter who I am or that he's never
seen me. Off-season, the boardwalk's empty pay phone rings

through the chemical Atlantic's curse and slap.
What can I say? Me, another stranger with empty pockets,

bad habits, unpacking my sequence of crises vanquished, surpassed
then spread upon the beach between us. He's staggered away

and it's as if I'm swimming in a theater's musk of plush,
watching myself drunk again on blanched sunlight, the lethal

hum of oleander, whatever ravening thing we want that's
so illusory. Los Angeles. The audience shuffles

while in the balcony a man weeps before the film commences.
That concrete arroyo I, someone not I, wandered once

through blurred frames to this two-bit Sonoran rodeo – everyone
swilling beer around a chestnut gelding, shoulders lathered,

his nostrils tortured to a rude facsimile of roses. Such breath,
such confounding brilliance, this slim Mexican saying *estrella,*

*estrellita,* fingering my blond hair. Maybe it was the sunglasses.
Or a tincture of sweat and panic like that streaking

the forehead of the B-movie actress playing someone's
discarded mistress down on a binge, reeling stupidly through

pastel hallucinated alleys seeking amnesia's salt tequila sting.
A stranger with formal collar and cummerbund. Someplace

where there are no casual encounters. But tonight, a continent away
there's the salt kiss, full on the mouth, of another ceaseless ocean

bestowing gnarled rafts of weed, the styrofoam and high heels.
I wasn't supposed to be in that arroyo. The Mexicans

weren't supposed to be in the country. Larger and larger
circles of not belonging, as if we belonged anywhere

marooned in our tidepools of tiaras and razors, little kits
brought along for the ride. As if anything, finally, belongs to us –

those intangible empires of fear and regret, sudden
crests of tenderness. Even the soul, some would hold,

escapes to a vast celestial band wrapping the world
without us. In Los Angeles, a beige froth of haze

hid the mountains. *Estrellita,* and what gone thing
did the Mexican recall in that turning? A girl's dusky hand

cradling fruit with silvery skin, coiled pulp the tint of roses
in mist? Or was it dust cascading from the tipped palm, La Pelona,

that old bald uncle, Death, spitting on a barroom floor?
In this movie time's running out. The Mexican touched my hair

and I took the kiss full on the mouth, sweet fruit, miraculous
chemistry of salts and water that keeps the flesh, that swells

and spills and feels so like weeping. What belongs to me,
if not this? Given splendor by the pay phone's luminescence,

the man wearing evening clothes slumps upon the boardwalk.
Perhaps he is the messenger beneath these chilling stars,

these heavenly infernos, burning here above the sea.

Confettied to shreds, the last leaves darken
       gusts that shrug passersby
into winter. On the sill, a fly's husk rattles
       its hollow cartouche, photos

spread across the table in this perishing slant
       of afternoon. Distant
with afterlife's opacity, my friend's face shadows
       the surface, so many cherished

strangers, the stolen kiss returned with its burden.
       Again, the struck chord
of some rapt entropic melody, the static fall
       of a kimono from alabaster

shoulders. Was it a blue room or a shade more sheer
       like gauze fluting the brow?
Was the white piano by the wall, crumbling plaster
       and ivy twining to espalier

the inside of this place, the mind's edge glimpsed
       by half-sleep? Calm is
apparitional at times like these, December's first
       gale from the sea rocking

this ship of a house in surge and creak, water
　　　　foaming the road. Before me,
the photos fan the hour's edge, my friend caught
　　　　like this – angle of bone,

aquiline bridge too visible through translucent skin.
　　　　Savage out there.
Fence pickets undo themselves from next-door's yard
　　　　where a television fills

with snow. Capricious nature, this uneasy providence,
　　　　and here's remembrance
arriving with the azure hiss of airmail letters:
　　　　blanketed in black and white,

he's propped in wicker, the crescent of beach dissolving
　　　　to sea behind him, the most
remote margin of land where on rare days it's possible
　　　　to walk endlessly, it seems,

into breakers, the tide . . . Beside him, an ashen
　　　　cyclamen. One failing stem
designs pure curve, the single bloom so like the shape
　　　　of cormorants in flight

beyond tawny estuaries, beyond rollers in the bay
        striking out like the shoulders of
so many swimmers. At first his mortal glance seems empty,
        then it's clear the emptiness

is mine, that half-dreamt room is grief, a single
        creased syllable opening
to the circling of cormorants inviolate, beyond
        the coast of anything we know.

Across Majestic Boulevard, *Steam Bath*
neons the snow to blue, and on her table
a blue cup steams, a rime of stale cream
circling its rim. Before finding the chipped case

behind the mirror, she waits for morning
the way an addict must wait, a little longer,
and studies the torn print on the wall –
lilies blurred to water stains, a woman

floating in a boat trailing fingers
in its wake. Someone rich. Someone gone.
Maybe a countess. She lets herself drift in the boat
warming thin translucent hands in coffee steam.

She's not a countess, only another girl
from the outer boroughs with a heroin habit as long
as the sea routes that run up and down the coast.
She's read all winter a life of Hart Crane, losing

her place, beginning again with Crane in a room
by the bridge, the East River, spending himself
lavishly. She's spent her night
circulating between piano bars and cabarets

where Greek sailors drink and buy her
cheap hotel champagne at 10 bucks a shot
before evaporating to another port on the map
of terra incognita the waterlilies chart

along her wall. The mantel is greened with
a chemical patina of sweat and time, and she can't
call any of this back. Hart Crane sways,
a bottle of scotch in one hand, his face plunged

inside the gramophone's tin trumpet, jazzed
to graceless oblivion. She rinses her face
in the basin, cold water, then turns to glance
across the boulevard where life's arranged

in all its grainy splendor. The steam bath sign
switches off with dawn, a few departing men
swathed in pea coats. The bath attendant climbs
as always to the roof, then opens the dovecote

to let his pigeons fly before descending to his berth.
They bank and curve towards the harbor that surrenders
to the sea. She knows Crane will leap
from the *Orizaba*'s stern to black fathoms

of water, that one day she'll lock this room
and lose the key. The gas flame's yellow coronet
stutters and she rolls her stocking down at last
to hit the vein above her ankle, until carried forward

she thinks it's nothing but the velocity of the world
plunging through space, the tarnished mirror
slanted on the mantel showing a dove-gray sky
beginning to lighten, strangely, from within.

★ II ★

Next, the dull silk thwack of an umbrella opening. No, that
was later, her grandmother's
hands & the umbrella smelled like some lost decade, like shelter –
camphor & lavender.
They're going to feed the swans, a long bus ride past
the wilderness of chrome
dinettes where soda jerks shimmy behind their blinding counters.
Tenements unpin themselves
from gray construction-paper sky dieseled to nothingness
by the bus's passage
to orange leaves pasting copper beeches in the park. There is

the door's pneumatic snap
behind them, then rain fuming the pavement, Indian summer
& couples loiter –
young men fatally cool in pointed shoes, leather jackets
wrapping the shoulders
of varnish-haired girls. Her grandmother holds
a sack of bread while
she kneels by the lake. Swans gloss towards shore & she sees
through her face in the shallows
by the sluice, a mask rippled over the bottom's plush ferment
of silt & leaves. Then silently,

the swans arrive opening & closing coral beaks, black tongues.
They cancel her reflection

with their cluster & jostle for crumbs. She knows about the gods,
how they come to earth sometimes
as swans. Dense mist rivulets snowy backs & her sweater is fog
when the slim necks arc over her
their soft, laddered clucking & what alien grace, the white weight
of swans leaving water
& for once she has no longing for the future, for beauty
beyond the trance of swans.
There's thunder & I know they all must leave the park for the heart's
violent destinations –
raptures & betrayals, departures & returns, a torrent
of stories bewildering

& arbitrary as any the gods might choose. In one,
war begins,
the swans are garroted with piano wire, a soldier
unraveling his skein
of private nightmares. Her grandmother saves the clipping.
Another has the girl
argue with her grandmother, take flight to suffer, almost
accidentally, her first kiss.
The darkened park. This utter stranger. But here the stories
blur until the soldier is
the stranger & the hands that tangle the girl's damp hair, tilt back
a long swan's neck, so rippling
transformed, she's reflected in that stricken human face trying

to lose itself over hers
in a ferment of white wings, sluice-water dousing park lights.

So many seasons' debris, where the crumbs she'd strewn
as a child vanish again,
chimerical as memory, & swans glide away carving
clear wakes in a timeless
still lake. I see a girl waiting for a bus.
Lightly, it's raining
on her grandmother's face so the umbrella opens its scent
& bus tickets stain
their hands with minute, indigo numbers that show the fare.

From the hospital solarium we watch row houses
change with evening down the avenue, the gardener

bending to red asters, his blond chrysanthemums.
Each day I learn more of the miraculous.

The gardener rocks on his heels and softly
Riva talks to me about the d.t.'s, her gin

hallucinations. The willow on the lawn
is bare, almost flagrant in the wind off

Baltimore harbor. She wants me to brush her hair.
Some mornings I'd hear her sing to herself

numbers she knew by heart
from nightclubs on the waterfront circuit.

I wondered if she watched herself dissolve
in the mirror as shadows flickered, then whispering

gathered. Floating up the airshaft
her hoarse contralto broke over "I Should Care,"

"Unforgettable," and in that voice
everything she remembered – the passage

from man to man, a sequence of hands
undressing her, letting her fall like the falling

syllables of rain she loves, of steam, those trains
and ships that leave. How she thought for years

a departure or a touch might console her, if only
for the time it takes luck to change, to drink

past memory of each stranger that faltered
over her body until her song was a current

of murmurs that drew her into sleep, into
the shapes of her fear. Insects boiling

from the drain, she tells me, a plague
of veiled nuns. Her hair snaps, electric

in the brush, long, the color of dust or rain
against a gunmetal sky. I saw her once, at the end

of a sullen July dusk so humid that the boys
loitering outside the Palace Bar & Grill

moved as if through vapor. She was reeling
in spike heels, her faded blue kimono.

33

They heckled her and showered her with pennies,
spent movie tickets. But she was singing.

That night I turned away and cursed myself
for turning. She holds a glass of water

to show her hands have grown more steady.
*Look,* she whispers, and I brush

and braid and the voices of visiting hour rise
then wind like gauze. The gardener's flowers nod,

pale in the arc lamps that rinse the factory boys
shooting craps as they always do down on

Sweet Air Avenue. I know they steam the dice
with breath for luck before they toss,

and over them the air shimmers the way still water
shimmers as gulls unfold like Riva's evening hands

across the sky, tremulous, endangered.

A floating city of substance, of ether
    and haze, the great liner crests and breaks through
        foam, streams of cold turquoise. On deck,
slippery, wet, deserted at six in the morning
    *tall deck chairs rest in rows with their knees up*

*to their chins,* I write on blue onionskin,
    a letter home. *My ninth day on the ocean*
        *and we're almost to Havre. By noon*
*we'll be off the boat and on the train –*
    Paris, the radiant destination.

I mouth its syllables, the name *Millay,* and think
    I'll change my name to *Violette.*
        Long before dawn, awake from restless half-sleep
I kept watch to see the sky rinse then pearl
    through the porthole, but no, and the whole ship

was sleeping, lingerie frothing from steamer trunks
    in watery light, cut iris on nightstands.
        Even the rats slumbering in the granary
or among the nervous legs of racehorses.
    Last night off starboard Laurence pointed towards

lighthouses, the Cornish coast, and I thought I'd die
    thinking of Tristan and Iseult, their story

of rue and devotion and we were there
held in the same chill current, a couple
    with scotch on our breaths and I leaned over

the railing where waves churned, obscuring the glimmer
    of Cornwall then showing again the visible present
        streamed into myth, cold turquoise. Nine days at sea –
a floating city – and in the ship's grand ballroom
    the journey's last fête careened, everyone

chattering in French champagned beneath
    the chandeliers. Mademoiselle Simone's mynah slipped
        his gold leg chain and fluttered from table to table,
awkward on lopped wings shrieking *bloody pack*
    *of knaves* in dockside Limey English

so the orchestra cranked louder to drown
    him out but everyone was drunk and didn't care.
        Is it wrong, this craze for Europe,
this vast grand fling, all of us flooding from America,
    the crass and gaudy, towards what farther shore?

Beauty? A form of love or devotion?
    Thin arabesques of laughter, the sudden gash
        of a badly painted mouth. Outside

the deck dropped then crested like the roller coaster
in Maine when I was a child – four stories tall –

the white roller coaster and through trees far below
people strolled in straw hats and beyond the park
the summer glitter of the same sea that frosted me
past midnight still warm and giddy from the ballroom.
Salt mist crimped my hair, the blanket Laurence wrapped

around my shoulders. Tristan, wounded, crossed
the Channel, maybe here, for Brittany and I
shiver into the traveler's extravagant
elation veined with fear. Paris, the radiant destination.
I wanted to see the day break over France

but the sun won't rise at all this morning
because it's raining. Nine days at sea
and this early I'm alone for once on deck
*a minor jazz-age duenna* without the rainbow-colored
dress of scarves, no entourage of sloe-eyed flappers,

no flaming youths, only this solitary sway over
cold marine depths, sunken crystal. The ship's
a floating city of ether and haze awash
in bands of sea and sky that merge. Was there rain
or sunlight when Tristan writhed with fever

waiting for the longboat which carried Iseult?
　　Black sail, white sail, a confusion of sails.
　　　　Tristan and Iseult each longing to be touched,
transformed, to be one and never, never,
　　always that distance, that illusive

deceiving horizon. He suffers time the way
　　a lover always will, a traveler, as if
　　　　by having at last the loved one, as if
by merely arriving a completion takes place.
　　The harrowed waves. Paris, the destination

an irreal embrace of starlight twenty-four hours
　　a day, white monuments gracing fragrant
　　　　boulevards. The cabin steward wants to know
if I'm cold but I don't care because the drop
　　of the deck is the white roller coaster

swinging over the sea, that stark
　　delicious vertigo and people
　　　　way below sipping lemonade with mint.
The steward shakes my shoulder, then with the bow
　　and flourish of a cabaret emcee

says, *Voilà, la terre de France,* and I stare
　　and stare a long time, not even thinking

and I don't care if it rains while the great liner
cruises these glorious, numbered hours.
   The car, the car would hesitate then tilt as it lurched

to descend past hurtling signs – *Hold Your Hat,*
   *Don't Stand,* at each turn, *Don't Let Go,*
      and I know I will never arrive.

Below the viaduct, the 5:05's stiff wind snares
the whole block in its backlash, and although
the morning fairly aches with promise, only
insomniacs are out, the million-dollar dreamers
orphaned by love's chameleon reversals.
What joins me to my neighbor is this

silent complicity: by flashlight I uproot
dandelions and crabgrass, while on his fire escape
he does calisthenics. A month ago he came home
to an empty flat and that emptiness turns
its dull blade inside his chest. Caught by the last
anemic sickle of moon, perhaps he thinks himself

more than half a man, but less than full.
This early the street's washed black and white,
jittery as a sixteen-millimeter reel. It's easy
to understand, at times like this, the sudden
desire to commend oneself into the hands
of sympathetic strangers who, in certain

transfiguring lights, wear the faces of husbands
and wives. And then there's the edgy allure
of the dangerous ones – that red-haired cashier
with an emerald piercing her nostril's flare,

or the carnival boy who tends the shooting booth —
those blind ducks with rings painted round

their necks. This business of being human
should not be such a lonely proposition. Maybe
I should drop my spade and stride
to my neighbor's alley, call out, *It is I,*
*the one for whom you have been waiting.*
*Come down. Let us join our forces.* Yes,

a brash tarantella through fireweed, the shattered
bottle glass. But I am not so bold, not nearly
so presuming. Instead I note the snail's
slimy progress and my neighbor touches toes
until the fog rolls down the hill like a memory
that wants losing. He performs deep knee bends

until he strikes a contract with himself
that gets him through his day, a deal not unlike
the one between earth and root, between
green pear and empty hand. My neighbor
crawls back through his window, his landing
sways its vacant iron grid, and above

the plummeting alley, a sleek gray seam of sky.
Pretty soon deals will go down all over the city.

The fruit vendor will appear singing strawberries
and watermelons. From their tanks, lobsters
in the seafood markets will wave pincers as if
imploring the broken factory clock that registers

9:99 in the morning, o° even in the heart of summer.
Answer me. What am I to make of these signs?

Soot-blackened, marble angels freeze
  their serpentine ascent above scattered women
    in the pews, net shopping bags beside them as

the priest drones mass before an altar carbonized
  with Madrid's incessant traffic fumes. In stone,
    the Virgin rests her foot upon the serpent

coiling a benighted world, and tarnished
  in their reliquary, the hermit's fingers play
    no instrument but incensed air. Such a meager

gathering, yet here is the visionary beggar riding
  tissued layers of soiled garments, notebook
    in her hands, transcribing helplessly

her transport in a code of suns and doves'
  entrails, crouched seraphim. Because he believed
    the mad inhabited zones of heaven, El Greco

painted in asylums — the saint's blue arms
  raised in rapture truly modeled from the madman's
    supplications. Cries and rough whispers,

nuns' habits sweeping across stone floors, disturbing
   the stacks of charcoal studies. He found derangement
     spiritual. The cathedral font is dry today,

stained glass rattling the passage of Vespas
   and taxicabs. The stairway tumbles, Baroque,
     to the boulevard twitching with heat, gypsied with

cripples, the sots and marvelous dancing goats.
   In the Prado, Greco's attenuated aristocrat
     buys his way to grace beside a Virgin transfigured –

the Resurrection. What Calvary in the model's mind
   built that cathedraled radiance of her glance,
     so matte and dense and holy? They're everywhere

in these vivid streets living parallel
   phantasmic cities that shimmer and burn among
     swirling crowds along the esplanade – tangoing couples

dappled under trees, the fortune-tellers
   and summer girls like dropped chiffon scarves
     sipping their turquoise infusions, planetary liqueurs

sticky with umbrellas. They chatter through
   a dwarf's frantic homily of curses. Simply
      a ripple the crowd absorbs, but where is the saint

from the plains' walled city the tourists
   come to find? *Oh, she is broken on the wheel,*
      *milled into dust. She is atomized to history's*

*dry footnotes.* Here is the sleek plane's vapor,
   the speed-blind train, and there the fragrant secrets
      inside fine leather. Still, the painter shows the beggar's

empty bowl, irradiated shades, these gaseous figures
   writhing upward, hands knotting tremulous prayers.
      And the mouths, the mouths . . . Such hollow caverns

that plumb what depths of human pain, or is it
   ecstasy's abandon? Past a twilight the color of sighs
      on the street made numinous with restaurant lights,

he is there, the man kneeling before a shopfront's
   iron grille. Facing, rapt, a silk-swathed mannequin,
      he's chanting litanies in a perfumed tongue

of numerals, some unearthly lexicon. And if we could
translate, we might hear how the saint dwells
perpetual, the form of this hunger within.

# ★ Utopia Parkway ★

after Joseph Cornell's *Penny Arcade Portrait of Lauren Bacall, 1945–46*

Marble steps cascade like stereopticon
frames of quays along the Seine he's ready
to descend, a folio beneath his arm
of yellowed pages wreathed in the aura of French,
a cache of star maps and movie stills, Lauren Bacall.

Parisian breezes siphon off into slight vacuums
left in air by the passage of young men
wheeling racks of suits and dresses towards
the Garment District. New York and the twilit
Public Library steps where each instant spins

a galaxy of signs – the flushed marquees
and newsboys' shouts fold into hoarse cries, street vendors
of former times when parrots picked fortune cards
from drawers beneath their hurdy-gurdy cages
outside Coney Island's Penny Arcade. Towards

Times Square, streaming taillights weave nets of connections
carmine as Bacall's lipsticked pout in *Screenplay
Magazine,* and the whole bedazzled city's
a magnificent arcade one might arrange in a cabinet,
those amusement-park contraptions worked by coins

or tinted wooden balls traveling runways
to set into motion compartment

after compartment, a symphony of sight and sound
into fantasy, into the streets of New York through
Oriental skies, until the balls come to rest

in their tray releasing a shower of prizes:
A milliner's illuminated display of hats,
the stamp hat tilted over Bacall's arched eyebrows, filings
spread across the inspector's desk, her sullen gaze.
On Utopia Parkway, in his workshop, Bacall's

dossier's lain for months untouched among springs
and dolls' heads, ballerinas arcing through
charted celestial spheres, that music.
Hoagy Carmichael's heard offstage as he threads
the rush-hour crowd. A typist's crooked stocking seams

recall with affection the actress on her way up –
the modeling jobs, ushering in New York. The box will work
by a rolling ball wandering afield into childhood,
an insight into the lives of countless young women
who never knew, may never know, any other home

than the plainest of furnished rooms, a drab hotel.
The drama of a room by lamplight, hotel neon
in *To Have and Have Not*. Carmichael's "Hong Kong Blues,"

blue glass like the night-blue of early silent films –
an atmosphere of cabaret songs, "How Little We Know."

Fog, the boat scenes, and each compartment becomes
a silver screen. Offstage music, and now we hear
the music in Cornell's eternity as the actress
takes her place among the constellations,
Cygnus, the Pleiades, one of the Graces.

Someone's saying it's almost time for the ambulance.
Then there's your own shocked face
in the Public Bathroom's mirror, already underwater,
the woman curled at your feet, foam speckling her lips.
Beyond these sinks, towards blind pavillions
escalators lunge briefcases, scented fur coats
conveyed above mental patients set loose upon the town.
Counterfeit daylight thrums the upper platform's
bland heaven. Familiar numbered streets erase themselves –
your ride uptown – 14th, 23rd, 42nd, counting into the concourse
swarmed with zero-hour losers, newsprint, incense,
that Haitian lynx cooing her rich patois, hawking charms for
    nightmare's
hexed recurrent voodoo. Counterfeit daylight.

The *No* clenched inside. On the tiles, the woman whose throat
is ringed with bandannas, whose collapse is a stain you want
to step around. Shove your hands deep inside your pockets
and make like you're cool about the few decisions away she lays
beneath the cascade of endless running faucets. Someone's
calling for an ambulance. Where is your room, lucid
sunlight fanning rooftops? Where is the subway stop
named *Esperanza*? No, that was another country.
Hope, safe haven against the riptide's snarling wake. A heaven
vast, impersonal. So where are the angels of Reckoning
and Assuagement to hold this woman's hand, thin fingers

splayed against the tiles beneath her many coats?
And you're part of this, Doll, by the indifferent turn
of an ankle, the glance casually averted. Let's say
once she believed in human goodness among these blind pavillions.

This woman. Lie down with her, nestle your face
in retch and tremor, her rank hair. Palm her temples.
Lie down in the whir of roofs lifting away as you knew
they always must, clamorous pauses between marquees and
     parking lots
filled with an ascension of pigeons. Shall those who'll
die, like her, so publicly, hear the underneath of plosive secret
     voices?
How up and down the island buildings bulge and sob, the great
tailor's shears above Varick Street clipping endlessly the thread
that holds all of this together, these partial stories overheard:

           *Chestnuts steaming on a brazier,*
*yes . . .*
        *Play a tenspot,*
                 *Silverice in the eighth . . .*
*The 5:12,*
           *missing that, the 5:28 . . .*
*We always liked . . .*

*The mind has precincts of pain, exiles*
*within the precincts of pain . . .*

So, listen now with her to this broken wake of commuters
safe in their passage, always passing. And who bears responsibility?
Only angels of Fraud and Dissembling
tinsel the Strip tonight, a ceaseless run of water
from busted taps telling how it felt as she let go,
fingers loosening, her many clothes unfurling. Dante's Grove
of Suicides, you think. But no. Allusions break down.
She'd have nothing but contempt for you, guilty and standing here
long past the last train, waiting for the police sweep,
waiting for the clamp on the wrist, concrete sweating against your
    forehead.
It's almost time for the sirens to begin, the shaking,
a trembling from within.

42nd, 23rd, 14th counting backwards, so when at last
the Haitian arrives to press earth into your hands, a rubble
of bone and charms, you'll go down on your knees, willing to pay,
and keep on paying. Wasn't this exactly what you wanted?

A woman, after an absence of many years, returns
    to her old neighborhood and finds it a little more
        burned, more abandoned. Through rooftop aerials

the stadium's still visible where the boys of summer
    spun across the diamond and some nights she'd hear
        strikes and pop flies called through the open windows

of the rooms she shared with a man she thought
    she loved. All that summer, she watched
        across the street the magician's idiot son

paint over and over the Magic & Costume Shop's
    intricate portico – all frets and scallops, details
        from another century. The more he painted though

the more his sheer purity of attention seemed
    to judge her own life as frayed somehow and wrong.
        Daily the son worked until the city swerved

towards night's dizzy carnival with moons
    and swans afloat in neon over the streets.
        One evening she saw the magician's trick bouquet

flower at the curb while he filled his car.
   He folded the multicolored scarves, then
      caged the fabulous disappearing pigeons.

It is a common human longing to want utterly
   to vanish from one life and arrive transformed
      in another. When the man came home, he'd

touch her shoulders, her neck, but each touch
   discovered only the borders of her solitude.
      As a child in that neighborhood she'd believed

people were hollow and filled with quiet music, that
   if she were hurt deeply enough she would break
      and leave only a blue scroll of notes.

At first when he hit her, her face burned.
   Far off the stadium lights crossed the cool
      green diamond and burnished cobwebs swaying

on the ceiling. Then she became invisible,
   so when the doctor leaned over and asked
      her name all she could think of were her dresses

thrown from the window like peonies exploding
   to bloom in the clear dark air. No music –
      merely a rose haze through her lids, something

ticking in her head like a metronome
   in a parlor, dusty and arid with steam heat.
      How many lives she'd passed through to find

herself, an aging woman in black, before the locked
   and empty shop. So much sleight of hand, the years
      simply dissolving. Again she hears the crowd,

a billow of applause rippling across the brilliant
   diamond, across the mysterious passage
      of time and the failure of sorrow to pass away.

Of course there's the rose
tranced across sun-warmed tile,

but also the soft tattoo
of newsprint along a commuter's palm,

the flush of a motel sign the instant
it signals No Vacancy. I have always loved

these moments of delicate transition:
waking alone in a borrowed house

to a slim meridian of dawn barring
the pillow before the cool breeze,

a curtain of rain on the iron steps, rain
laving lawn chairs arranged

for a conversation finished days ago.
The Japanese call this *utsuroi,*

a way of finding beauty at the point
it is altered, so it is not the beauty

of the rose, but its evanescence
which tenders the greater joy.

Beneath my hands the cat's thick fur
dapples silver, the slant of afternoon.

How briefly they flourish then turn,
exalted litanies in the rifts

between milliseconds, time enough for a life
to change, and change utterly.

The magnesium flash of headlights
passing backlit the boy's face

in my novel – the heroine's epiphany
and she knows she is leaving, a canopy

of foliage surrounds his dark hair
whispering *over, over* – that sweet rending.

Nothing linear to this plot, simply
the kaleidoscopic click and shift

of variations undone on the instant:
evening as it vanishes gilds

the chambermaid's thin blond hair
in her hotel window and she thinks

*I could die now, and it would be enough.*
Long beyond nightfall, after the café's closing

the waiters slide from their jackets and set
places for themselves, paper lanterns blowing

in the trees, leaf shapes casting and recasting
their fugitive spell over the tables,

over the traffic's sleek sussurrus.

★ III ★

So easily you fall to sleep, the room a cage of rain,
the wallpaper's pinstripe floral another rift
between us, this commerce of silences and mysteries
called marriage, but that's not what this is about.

It's this wet balcony, filigreed, this rusty fan of spikes
the pensione's installed against thieves and this weather –

needling rain that diminuendoes into vapor, fog
dragging its cat's belly above the yellow spikes
of leaves, the hungry map the hustlers make stitching through
the carnival crowd below, and I'm thinking of Picasso's

early work – an exhibit of childhood notebooks, a *Poetics'*
margins twisting with doves and bulls and harlequins. Your face,

our friends', the sullen milling Spaniards, repeated canvases
of faces dismantled, fractured so as to contain
the planar flux of human expression – boredom to lust
and fear, then rapture and beyond. He was powerless,

wasn't he, before all that white space? I mean he had to
fill it in, and I can fill in the blank space of this room

between you and me, between me and the raucous promenade,
with all the rooms and galleries I've known, now so wantonly

painting themselves across this room, this night, the way
I extend my hand and the paseo, foreign beyond my fingertips,

dissolves to a familiar catastrophe of facades, the angles
of walls and ceilings opening all the way to the waterfront

where the standard naked lightbulb offers its crude flower
of electricity to blue the dark abundant hair a woman
I could have been is brushing, a torn shade rolled up to see
the bird vendor's cat upon his shoulder or, at some other stage

in their pursuit, the same French sailor I see drunkenly
courting the queen dolled up in bedsheet and motorcycle chain,

some drag diva strung out on something I can't name, something
kicking like this vicious twin inside who longs to walk
where guidebooks say not to, who longs to follow beyond all
common sense, that childhood love of terror propelling us

through funhouses and arcades, mother of strange beauty and faith.
But it's only chill rain that gathers in my palm, the empty

terra-cotta pots flanking the balcony. Rain and the ache
in my hands today, those off-tilt Gaudis queasily spelling
the tilt from port to port any life describes: Boston's damp cold
and we're stuffing rags again in broken windows, that condemned

brownstone on harshly passionate – Mr. Lowell – Marlborough
   Street
where our feet skimmed, polished black across the floor,

damp, the tattered hems of trousers. Simply trying like always
to con our way to some new dimension. And weren't we glamorous?
Oh, calendar pages riffling in the artificial wind
of some offscreen fan, a way to show life passing, the blurred

collage of images we collect to show everything and nothing
has changed. But I want to talk about the swans of Barcelona

this afternoon in the monastery pool, battered palms
and small bitter oranges smashed against pavement stones.
And those swans, luxurious and shrill by turns. It's not swans
that arrest me now – only this sailor staggering on the paseo

fisting the air between him and the queen, shouting *je sens, je sens,*
but he isn't able to say what he feels any more than I understand

how it is that perspective breaks down, that the buried life
wants out on sleepless nights amidst these coils of citizens,
a carnival dragon snaking, sodden, through the trees above them.
I know. I know, there's got to be more than people ruthlessly

hurricaned from port to port. I know tomorrow is a prayer
that means hope, that now you breathe softly, sleeping face

rent by sooted shadows the thief's grille throws while you're
turned into whatever dream you've made of these curious days
filled with cockatoos and swans, the endless rain.
Things get pretty extreme, then tomorrow little blades

of grass will run from silver into green
down the esplanade where a waiter places

ashtrays on the corners of tablecloths
to keep them firmly anchored.
The drag queen will be hustling, down on her knees
in the subway, a few exotic feathers twisting in the wind.

But it won't be me, Jack. It won't be me.

Past midnight, September, and the moon dangles
mottled like a party lantern about to erupt
in smoke. The first leaves in the gutter eddy,
deviled by this wind that's traveled years,

whole latitudes, to find me here believing
I smell the fragrance of mock orange. For weeks
sometimes, I can go without thinking of you.
Crumpled movie handbills lift then skitter

across the pavement. They advertise the one
I've just seen – "Drunken Angel" – Kurosawa's
early film of occupied Japan, the Tokyo slums
an underworld of makeshift market stalls

and shacks where Matsu, the consumptive gangster,
dances in a zoot suit to a nightclub's swing band.
The singer mimes a parody of Cab Calloway
in Japanese. And later, as Matsu leans coughing

in a dance-hall girl's rented room, her painted
cardboard puppet etches shadows on the wall
that predict his rival's swift razor
and the death scene's slow unfurling, how

he falls endlessly it seems through a set
of doors into a heaven of laundry: sheets
on the line, the obis and kimonos stirring
with his passage. And all of this equals

a stark arithmetic of choices, his fate
the final sum. Why must it take so long
to value what's surrendered so casually?
I see you clearly now, the way you'd wait

for me, flashy beneath the Orpheum's
rococo marquee in your Hong Kong hoodlum's
suit, that tough-guy way you'd flick
your cigarette when I was late. You'd consult

the platinum watch, the one you'd lose
that year to poker. I could find again our room
above the Lucky Life Café, the cast-iron district
of sweatshop lofts. But now the square's deserted

in this small midwestern town, sidewalks
washed in the vague irreal glow of shopwindows,
my face translucent in the plate glass.
I remember this the way I'd remember a knife

against my throat: that night, after
the overdose, you told me to count, to calm
myself. You put together the rice-paper lantern
and when the bulb heated the frame it spun

shadows – dragon, phoenix, dragon and phoenix
tumbling across the walls where the clothes
you'd washed at the sink hung drying on
a nailed cord. The mock orange on the sill

blessed everything in that room
with its plangent useless scent. Forgive me.
I am cold and draw my sweater close. I discover
that I'm counting, out loud, in Chinese.

# ★ Carnival ★

Barcelona

Sure the advertisements are full of advice. They beseech
      everyone to get drunk or go
on vacation, to keep journeying to fill the wrenched vacancy,
      keep moving forward to find out

what's behind us – old news. By now the bird vendors are out
      dealing cockatoos and jeweled finches,
ringed pigeons, corrosively iridescent with morning.
      It's true the architecture's complex,

but sometimes I get fed up with swallowing diesel
      and cruising around in someone else's idea
of the good life. So here I am counting the hairs I've lost,
      while on the promenade people air

their ocelots beneath balconies festooned with streamers,
      confetti staining a turbaned sheik
three stories high bowing over a couple who've been up all night.
      The woman rolls a cigarette, blows smoke

while the man, wearing a lush's face, looks down at the table,
      hands over his eyes. Think I'll just
stay here to contemplate the defects of my own character,
      the pressed tin ceiling a topographical map

tattooed across the brain – my little piece of the universe.
     I know the clubs are full of parrots
with fortunes to tell, fat women in magenta tutus flashing
     the vast marble expanses

of their backs and all of them saying, "Where you from?"
     Singapore, Bali, the Republic
of Wherever I Want to Be From. The pipes screech their burden
     and last night that wrecked chanteuse

from 1936 told me the story of Barcelona's anarchists, three times
     how they shot her nephew,
nine years old, for stealing a chair. You see he had it wrong.
     He should have destroyed the chair.

A joke's no laughing matter here. Maybe I should dye my hair,
     book up the coast to Marseilles,
down to Marrakesh. I want to say there's time. That I have
     no regrets. Maybe I'll take a stroll,

drop a coin and talk to someone about the way life seems
     a dream of anarchy on highways, through masques
and arcades, the jittery palpitations, torrents of which
     the present is composed. The carnival resumes,

Ferris wheels slicing circles in the sky. Pipes burst
        an explosion of birds. So, I'm leaning over
the railing counting the pickpockets, addressing you,
        the abstract "you" that's the sum of everyone

I've known or lost or longed for. You know what I mean.
        What I want you to tell me
is how are we to fit between these palaces of justice
        and the waterfront's

bedraggled carnival? Or that ramshackle museum
        with cracked and muzzy skylights,
pots carefully arranged to catch the rain? Artifacts,
        I swear to you, disappeared before my eyes.

After the ribboning fever of interstate, after freight yards
& tinsel-towns, through the cranked-up mojo of radio signals,
through the moteled drift of nonsleep, comes the arms crossed

over the chest, the mind's blind odometer clicking backwards,
comes sifting over years the musk of those opened crates spilling

into that room, the abandoned building. Just me & him. Comes
the torn Army jacket & Detroit voice, dusky, the sweat-grayed
tee-shirt. A cup of snow-water melted on the ledge. No light –

simply candles pooled in wax across the floor, nothing more, but
those crates of rose crystal, hot out the backdoor of some
   swank shop.

While shadows flickered bare lathes, while he spasmed
the strung-out toss of too much hunger, too long, I set out
the beautiful *idea* of feast. Rose crystal plates & saucers

lined the mattress's thin margin of floor, guttering flames,
those teacup rims. Just me & him, that nameless jacket,

olive drab. I wanted to catch the cries, the ragged breath, how
we used to say come the revolution we'd survive anything, anything,
& condemned to that frugal repast we were, somehow, free.

Snow-water melted in the cup rinsed his forehead, that pure
juncture of clavicle & shoulder. Better this immersion

than to live untouched. I wanted to be the cup & flame,
I wanted to be the cure, the hand that held the river back
that would break us, as in time, we broke each other. Wait.

Not yet. While great newspresses crashed over next day's
headlines, while alley cats stalled beyond the wrenched police-lock

in a frieze of ferocious longing, his arms clenched the flawless
ache of thigh, damp curls. No clinic til break of day to break
the stream of fever I rocked with him towards the story I told

as a girl: the perfect city, luminous in the back of the radio,
jazz turned down so low it ghosted improvisations that let me fly

immune above skyscrapers, the endless gleaming arguments
of streets. I set out the platter, a delicate tureen & then
we *were* spark & fever, all frequencies tuned until

that piss-poor stinking room seemed shouldered through torn
    skyline.
Through spark & fever, shouldered beyond the folly of others

set adrift: the room of the girl who bends to gas flame deciding
coffee or suicide, beyond Roxbury's Emperor of Byzantium
alone on his Murphy-bed throne, tinfoil minarets & domes.

Condemned & oddly free, my hand following his ribs' dark curve,
the ridge of muscle there & there. James, what's the use?

After the broken arpeggios of all these years, comes this waking,
this stooping to the gas flame, comes the learning & relearning
through the long open moan of highway going on towards

a stream of crimson lifting away from the horizon. I wanted to
be the hand that held back the river, destiny. Comes this new day

cruelly, unspeakably rich, as that drenched grisaille of morning
came pouring then over blackened wicks, over all that crystal
fired empty & clean. Better this immersion than to live untouched.

No grand drama, only Chinatown's incendiary glow,
me returning to the old delinquent thrill of us

passing through this jimmied door, the herbalist's
shop gone broke & latticed with accordion grille.

Are these faces of ours oddly gentled, First Husband,
as evening's verge spills over bad-news gang-boys

filling vestibules with their bored sangfroid, over
old women smoothing newsprint sheets for carp steamed

to feathers of flesh? Two doors down, the gold-toothed
Cantonese lifts her tray of pastries streaming

red characters for sweet lotus, bitter melon, those
for fortune, grief, for marriage & rupture.

In my wallet, the torn wedding picture sleeps –
your brilliantine & sharkskin, my black-brimmed hat,

a cluster of glass cherries. Too young. Words roil
to calligraphy above us, cold as the dawn

your second wife wakes to, day-old rice then scorched
fluorescence through sweatshops, through bobbins

& treadles, the 6¢ piecework. When it's time,
we'll exchange a formal kiss in the whorling updraft

of burnt matches & apothecary labels, gang graffiti
slashed upon the walls. Why return to this empty shop

where I'd meet you sometimes after-hours over poker,
men chanting numbers in a sinuous grammar of 40-watt light

& smoke? Not much here now, a few drafty rooms, broken
drams of pungent White Flower Oil you'd rub my feet with,

bruised from dancing six sets a night between the star acts.
Not much, but what I choose to shape sleepless nights

far from here, when I'm diaphanous, engulfed again
by Chinatown's iron lintels, the hiss & spill of neon fog,

heliotrope & jade unrolled against the pavement I'd walk
in filmy stockings, the impossible platform shoes. As if

I might find her here again, my lost incarnation fallen
from the opulent emptiness of nightclubs, those

restaurants tuxedoed in their hunger. No one could
translate such precise Esperanto. And so we linger

tiny, surviving protagonists briefly safe here
from the crowd's ruthless press, a fanfare

of taxis polishing the avenues. Whenever next
I meet you, I'll meet you here in the harsh

auroral radiance of the squad car's liquid lights.
Things have never been so essential. I have seen

businesses fold & open like paper lilies, & men
leave for Hong Kong, then return to lie down

again in crowded rooms, the way each of us
lies down with a lacquered maze of corridors

& places where those once loved unbearably wear
strangers' faces. You run your hand through the hair

you've dyed black to hide the gray & out
on the street, sweet-faced vandals arabesque

caught in a rain of trinkets, green cards, the lucky
one-eyed jacks. Beneath my fingers, the twisted

braille of hearts & knives incised upon
the counter works its spell until the herbalist

takes up his abacus once more to commence
the sum of unguents, of healing roots,

a measure of time, a calculation beyond all worth.

Chet Baker, Amsterdam, 1988

A single spot slides the trumpet's flare then stops
    at that face, the extraordinary ruins thumb-marked
with the hollows of heroin, the rest chiaroscuroed.
    Amsterdam, the final gig, canals & countless

stone bridges arc, glimmered in lamps. Later this week
    his Badlands face, handsome in a print from thirty
years ago, will follow me from the obituary page
    insistent as windblown papers by the black cathedral

of St. Nicholas standing closed today: pigeon shit
    & feathers, posters swathing tarnished doors, a litter
of syringes. Junkies cloud the gutted railway station blocks
    & dealers from doorways call *coca, heroina,* some throaty

foaming harmony. A measured inhalation, again
    the sweet embouchure, metallic, wet stem. Ghostly,
the horn's improvisations purl & murmur
    the narrow *strasses* of *Rosse Buurt,* the district rife

with purse-snatchers, women alluring, desolate, poised
    in blue windows, Michelangelo boys, hair spilling
fluent running chords, mares' tails in the sky green
    & violet. So easy to get lost, these cavernous

brown cafés. Amsterdam, & its spectral fogs, its
    bars & softly shifting tugboats. He builds once more
the dense harmonic structure, the gabled houses.
    Let's get lost. Why court the brink & then step back?

After surviving, what arrives? So what's the point
    when there are so many women, creamy callas with single
furled petals turning in & in upon themselves
    like variations, nights when the horn's coming

genius riffs, metal & spit, that rich consuming rush
    of good dope, a brief languor burnishing
the groin, better than any sex. Fuck Death.
    In the audience, there's always this gaunt man, cigarette

in hand, black Maserati at the curb, waiting,
    the fast ride through mountain passes, descending with
no rails between asphalt & precipice. Inside, magnetic
    whispering *take me there, take me.* April, the lindens

& horse chestnuts flowering, cold white blossoms
    on the canal. He's lost as he hears those inner voicings,
a slurred veneer of chords, molten, fingering
    articulate. His glance below Dutch headlines, the fall

"accidental" from a hotel sill. Too loaded. What do you do
   at the brink? Stepping back in time, I can only
imagine the last hit, lilies insinuating themselves
   up your arms, leaves around your face, one hand vanishing

sabled to shadow. The newsprint photo & I'm trying
   to recall names, songs, the sinuous figures, but facts
don't matter, what counts is out of pained dissonance,
   the sick vivid green of backstage bathrooms, out of

broken rhythms – and I've never forgotten, never –
   *this is the tied-off vein, this is 3 A.M. terror*
*thrumming, this is the carnation of blood clouding*
   *the syringe,* you shaped *summer rains across the quays*

*of Paris, flame suffusing jade against a girl's*
   *dark ear.* From the trumpet, pawned, redeemed, pawned again
you formed one wrenching blue arrangement, a phrase endlessly
   complicated as that twilit dive through smoke, applause,

the pale haunted rooms. Cold chestnuts flowering April
   & you're falling from heaven in a shower of eighth notes
to the cobbled street below & foaming dappled horses
   plunge beneath the still green waters of the Grand Canal.

Houseboats roll soft with morning's thin drizzle,
     gypsy colors muted
  as we pass to wander the arboretum's
intricate chill paths,
     oval disks naming trees in Dutch,
      the familiar grown

  exotic in this city built on land
     that is sea, where
  our reflections merge with buildings floating
upside-down. A coverlet
     of ground mist wraps our ankles, so we seem,
      for a moment, nearly

  aerial, incorporeal within the distant
     sough of foghorns,
  then the museum's zones of pure atmosphere, galleries
of trompe l'oeils,
     convex interiors, the underwater hush
      of voices. Rain steady

  against the skylights' frosted lozenges dapples
     floors and walls, until
  outside is inside and we move among the lit

chambers of genre paintings
lavish with detail, small parables
of *vanitas* – dust

circling the goblet's rim, half-empty, flies
swimming the burst pear's
nectar. Excess and transience: even in Vermeer,
a girl bending to
her lustrous task weighs palmfuls of pearls,
the Last Judgment pinned

behind her in aquatint. Books crumble from leather
bindings, and time glazes
the fish's iridescent scales – decay so palpable
it stains the clearing sky
of afternoon, late in this violent century,
in time of plague.

I've seen the shadow cross over young men, clustered
addicts in parks
where bronzed explorers survey the Atlantic's
cold immensities, measured
in parchments like these cartographer's fancies, a world
more mysterious,

perhaps more richly imagined. The wing of afternoon
    tilts duskward, ochered in
  brief splendor and all around the tender regard
of countless saints
    and virgins. The closing hour signals and we enter
    again our fragile lives,

  bridges and boulevards webbed overhead
    with trolley wires,
  a host of tiny colored lights electrified
like constellations
    to conjure time's strange torque, the instant pulsing
    to a life's span

  as we turn once more towards each shining
    arborvitae, towards
  evening gardens drenched in the radiant
calm hue of chamomile,
    this illusion of a universe,
      a proffered gift.

Frayed cables bear perilously the antiquated lift,
all glass and wrought-iron past each apartment floor
like those devices for raising and lowering
angels of rescue in medieval plays. Last night
the stairwell lamps flickered off and I was borne up
the seven floors in darkness, the lift a small lit

cage where I thought of you, of the Catholic souls
we envisioned once, catechism class, the saint
in her moment of grace transfigured as she's engulfed
in flames. The lift shivered to a halt above the shaft
and I was afraid for a moment to open the grille,
wanting that suspension again, the requiemed hum

of one more city going on without me – Cockney girls
with violet hair swirling among the businessmen
and movie ushers of Soho, sullen in their jackets.
All of them staving off as long as they can
the inevitable passing away, that bland euphemism
for death. But I can't shake this from my mind:

your face with its hollows against hospital linen.
Newark's empty asylum wings opened again this year
for the terminal cases. Each day another
strung-out welfare mother, the street-corner romeos

we used to think so glamorous, all jacked-up
on two-buck shots. It was winter when I last was home

and my mother found you on her endless dietician's
rounds, her heavy ring of keys. It was winter
when I saw you, Loretta, who taught me to curse
in Italian, who taught me to find the good vein
in the blue and yellow hours of our sixteenth year
among deep nets of shadows dragged through evening, a surf

of trees by the railway's sharp cinders. Glittering
like teen-dream angels in some corny AM song,
buoyed by whatever would lift us above the smoldering
asphalt, the shingled narrow houses, we must
have felt beyond all damage. Still what damage carried you
all these years beyond the fast season of loveliness

you knew before the sirens started telling your story
all over town, before the habit stole
the luster from your movie-starlet hair.
Little sister, the orderlies were afraid to
touch you. Tonight, the current kicks the lights
back on and there's the steady moan of the lift's

descent, the portion of what's left of this day
spread before me – stockings drying on the sill, the cool

shoulders of milk bottles – such small domestic salvations.
There was no deus ex machina for you, gone now
this half year, no blazing escape, though how many times

I watched you rise again, and again from the dead:
that night at the dealer's on Orange Street, stripping
you down, overdosed and blanched against the green linoleum,
ice and saline. I slapped you until
the faint flower of your breath clouded the mirror.
In those years I thought death was a long blue hallway

you carried inside, a curtain lifting at the end
in the single window's terrible soft breeze where
there was always a cashier ready to take your
last silver into her gloved hands, some dicey, edgy game.
Beneath the ward clock's round dispassionate face
there was nothing so barren in the sift from minute

to absolute minute, a slow-motion atmosphere dense
as the air of medieval illuminations with demons
and diaphanous beings. I only wished then
the cancellation of that hungering that turns us
towards the mortal arms of lovers or highways
or whatever form of forgetfulness we choose.

Your breath barely troubled the sheets, eyes closed,
perhaps already adrift beyond the body, twisting
in a tissue of smoke and dust over Jersey's
infernal glory of cocktail lounges and chemical plants,
the lonely islands of gas stations lining the turnpike
we used to hitch towards the shore, a moment

I want back tonight – you and me on the boardwalk,
the casino arcade closed around its pinball machines
and distorting mirrors. Just us among sea serpents,
and the reckless murmur of the sea. Watching stars
you said you could almost believe the world arranged

by a design that made a kind of sense. That night
the constellations were so clear it was easy
to imagine some minor character borne up
beyond judgment into heaven, rendered purely
into light. Loretta, this evening washes
over my shoulders, this provisional reprieve.

I've been telling myself your story for months
and it spreads in the dusk, hushing the streets, and there
you are in the curve of a girl's hand as she lights
her cigarette sheltered beneath the doorway's plaster
cornucopia. Listen, how all along the avenue trees
are shaken with rumor of this strange good fortune.

It snakes behind me, this invisible chain gang —
the aliases, your many faces peopling

that vast hotel, the past. What did we learn?
Every twenty minutes the elevated train,

the world shuddering beyond
the pane. It was never warm enough in winter.

The walls peeled, the color of corsages
ruined in the air. Sweeping the floor,

my black wig on the chair. I never meant
to leave you in that hotel where the voices

of patrons long gone seemed to echo in the halls,
a scent of spoiled orchids. But this was never

an elegant hotel. The iron fretwork of the El
held each room in a deep corrosive bloom.

This was the bankrupt's last chance, the place
the gambler waits to learn his black mare's

leg snapped as she hurtled towards the finish line.

\*    \*    \*

How did we live? Your face over my shoulder
was the shade of mahogany in the speckled

mirror bolted to the wall. It was never warm.
You arrived through a forest of needles,

the white mist of morphine, names for sleep
that never came. My black wig unfurled

across the battered chair. Your arms circled me
when I stood by the window. Downstairs

the clerk who read our palms broke the seal
on another deck of cards. She said you're my fate,

my sweet annihilating angel, every naked hotel room
I've ever checked out of. There's nothing

left of that, but even now when night pulls up
like a limousine, sea-blue, and I'm climbing the stairs,

keys in hand, I'll reach the landing and
you're there – the one lesson I never get right.

Trains hurtled by, extinguished somewhere
past the bend of midnight. The shuddering world.

Your arms around my waist. I never meant to leave.

\*   \*   \*

Of all of that, there's nothing left but a grid
of shadows the El tracks throw over the street,

the empty lot. Gone, the blistered sills,
voices that rilled across each wall. Gone,

the naked bulb swinging from the ceiling,
that chicanery of light that made your face

a brief eclipse over mine. How did we live?
The mare broke down. I was your fate, that

yellow train, the plot of sleet, through dust
crusted on the pane. It wasn't warm enough.

What did we learn? All I have left of you
is this burnt place on my arm. So, I won't

forget you even when I'm nothing but
small change in the desk clerk's palm, nothing

but the pawn ticket crumpled in your pocket,
the one you'll never redeem. Whatever I meant

to say loses itself in the bend of winter
towards extinction, this passion of shadows falling

like black orchids through the air. I never meant
to leave you there by the pane, that

terminal hotel, the world shuddering with trains.

## THE IOWA
## POETRY PRIZE WINNERS

1987
Elton Glaser, *Tropical Depressions*
Michael Pettit, *Cardinal Points*

1988
Mary Ruefle, *The Adamant*
Bill Knott, *Outremer*

1989
Terese Svoboda, *Laughing Africa*
Conrad Hilberry, *Sorting the Smoke*


## THE EDWIN FORD PIPER
## POETRY AWARD WINNERS

1990
Lynda Hull, *Star Ledger*
Philip Dacey, *Night Shift at the Crucifix Factory*